Facts About the Lynx

By Lisa Strattin

© 2019 Lisa Strattin

FREE BOOK

FREE FOR ALL SUBSCRIBERS

LisaStrattin.com/Subscribe-Here

BOX SET

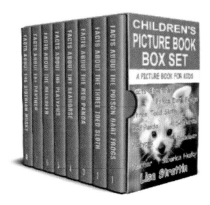

- **FACTS ABOUT THE POISON DART FROGS**
- **FACTS ABOUT THE THREE TOED SLOTH**
- **FACTS ABOUT THE RED PANDA**
- **FACTS ABOUT THE SEAHORSE**
- **FACTS ABOUT THE PLATYPUS**
- **FACTS ABOUT THE REINDEER**
- **FACTS ABOUT THE PANTHER**
- **FACTS ABOUT THE SIBERIAN HUSKY**

LisaStrattin.com/BookBundle

Facts for Kids Picture Books by Lisa Strattin

Little Blue Penguin, Vol 92

Chipmunk, Vol 5

Frilled Lizard, Vol 39

Blue and Gold Macaw, Vol 13

Poison Dart Frogs, Vol 50

Blue Tarantula, Vol 115

African Elephants, Vol 8

Amur Leopard, Vol 89

Sabre Tooth Tiger, Vol 167

Baboon, Vol 174

Sign Up for New Release Emails Here

LisaStrattin.com/subscribe-here

Contents

INTRODUCTION

The lynx is a member of the cat family and one of the larger felines of North America.

There are three different types of lynx: the North America Lynx found in Canada and Alaska, the European Lynx found in Spain and Portugal and the Asian Lynx which is found in Turkestan and central Asia.

CHARACTERISTICS

The North American Lynx is the biggest species of lynx and some of these animals have extremely thick and fluffy-looking fur, which keeps them warm in the freezing Canadian winter.

The European and Asian Lynx species are smaller in size and have personalities that resemble those of a domestic cat, rather than a large feline.

APPEARANCE

They are best known for their short stubby tails and the long tufts of black hair on their ears.

They have large paws which helps them to balance and also gives them more power when pursuing their prey. They also have acute hearing which allows them to hear oncoming prey and predators from far away. They also have a strong jaw and sharp teeth which are used to bite down on the prey when caught.

LIFESTYLE

Lynx are usually solitary animals and spend their time both hunting and resting alone. However a small group of them may travel and hunt together sometimes.

Lynx mating takes place in the late winter and the female will give birth to two to six kittens after a gestation period of about 70 days. The female will usually give birth to only one litter per year. The kittens stay with the mother for about nine months, so the mother cares for them over their first winter. The kittens then move out to live on their own as young adults. It is known that the adults will give their young prey to play with before they eat it; this thought to help develop their hunting skills.

LIFE SPAN

Lynx normally live for 12 to 20 years.

SIZE

An adult lynx is usually between 30 to 50 inches long and can weigh as much as 55 pounds.

HABITAT

The lynx tends to live in dense shrub and grassland areas in the forests of North America and parts of Eurasia.

They live in dens within rock crevices or under ledges that provides a safe place to rest as well as a home for their kittens. Usually, they do not take their kill back to their den, except when they are bringing food for the kittens.

DIET

Although the lynx is a ground mammal, they are known to climb trees or swim in water to catch their prey. They hunt small mammals, birds and fish but seem to prefer to hunt larger mammals like reindeer, deer and elk if these larger animals are in their native home range.

ENEMIES

Large meat-eating animals such as cougars and wolves are enemies that hunt and kill them. Coyotes, although relatively small, may also hunt them.

SUITABILITY AS PETS

A lynx is a wild animal is not meant to be kept as a pet or animal companion. Unless one is injured and cannot be rehabilitated and returned to the wild, they're best left alone in their natural habitats.

There are some wild animal sanctuaries that keep them, but these habitats likely have to apply for a special exotic animal license in order to do so. You can probably see a lynx in your local zoo, if you want to watch them up close.

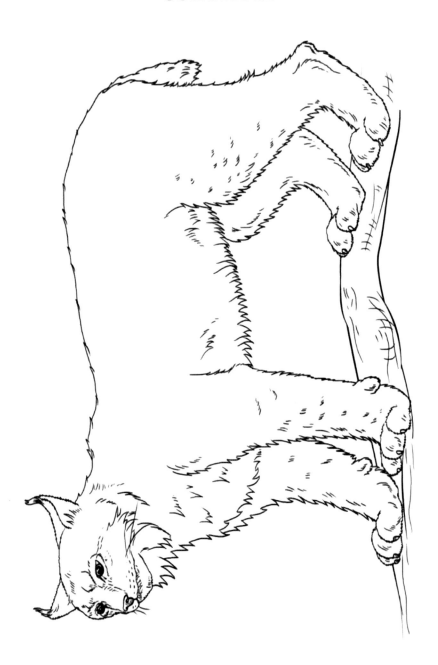

COLOR ME

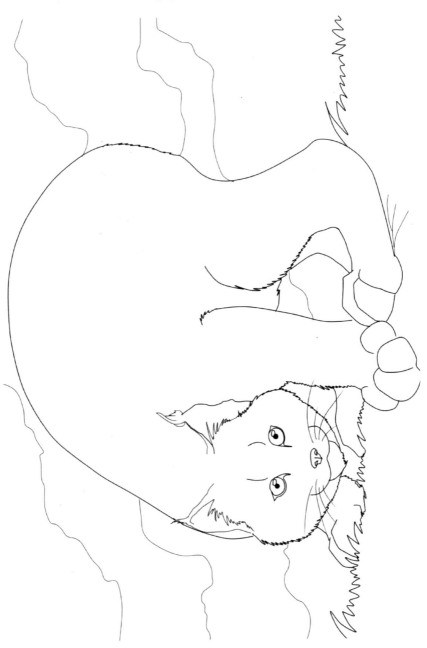

COLOR ME

COLOR ME

COLOR ME

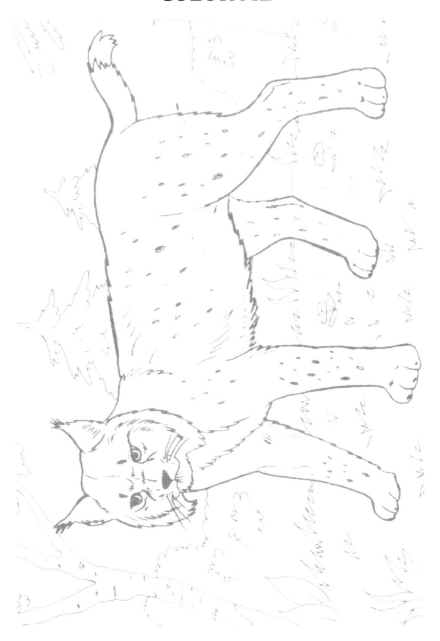

Please leave me a review here:

LisaStrattin.com/Review-Vol-278

For more Kindle Downloads Visit Lisa Strattin
Author Page on Amazon Author Central

amazon.com/author/lisastrattin

To see upcoming titles, visit my website at
LisaStrattin.com– most books available on Kindle!

LisaStrattin.com

FREE BOOK

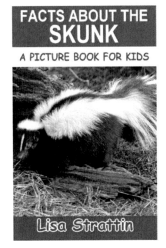

Made in the USA
Middletown, DE
12 January 2022

58482701R00024